I0162612

A

People Prepared

For the Lord

Dr. Dorothy Batts

A People Prepared for the Lord
Copyright ©2013 by Dr. Dorothy Batts
ISBN: 978-0-9884899-5-0
First Edition
Printed in the United States of America

2 4 6 8 10 9 7 5 3 1

Cover design by DNA Media
Interior layout and editing by D. Renee Gibbs

All scriptures taken from the King James Version
of the Holy Bible
Ryrie Study Bible Copyright
© 1986, 1994
THE MOODY BIBLE INSTITUTE OF CHICAGO
PILGRIM STUDY BIBLE – OXFORD UNIVERSITY
©2003

Published by:
Cranberry Quill Publishing, Inc.
111 Lamon Street, Suite 201, Fayetteville, NC 28301
www.cranberryquill.com

TABLE OF CONTENTS

PREFACE
Foundation of God Standeth Sure

Special section for taking notes following Chapter XIII

I am only the writer…Jesus is the author and finisher of my faith and also every book I write and every message I preach and teach.

Dr. Dorothy Batts

PREFACE
A People Prepared for the Lord

*"And many of the children of Israel shall he turn to the
Lord their God."*
Luke 1:16

*"And it shall come to pass in the last days, said God; I
will pour out of my Spirit upon all flesh: and your sons
and your daughters shall prophesy, and your young men
shall see visions, and your old men shall dream dreams."*
Acts 2:17

*"And on my servants and on my handmaidens I will
pour out in those days of my Spirit; and they shall
prophesy." Acts 2:18*

We are living in the last days. This is the day when
God is pouring out His Spirit upon all flesh. We are
also living in a day with those who have made their
minds up that they will not allow anything to separate
them from the Lord; even though they will encounter
trouble.

In the midst of the trouble, God is with us; and it is
the Lord who will lead us from trouble to triumph.
Many times it is the trouble that leads us into
triumph. It is also the trouble that prepares us for the
Lord. I did not understand this principle when I

became a born-again Christian and was translated out of the kingdom of darkness into Kingdom of God's dear Son. It is God who delivered us and we are delivered. Paul wrote in *Colossians1:13, "Who hath delivered us from the power of darkness, and hath translated us into the kingdom of his dear Son."*

I do not think my mentors knew these principles that God taught me. The way God taught me was by allowing me to live in the midst of the world of darkness and have a kingdom mind with the light of God. A kingdom mind is the mind of Christ.

What I am writing to you is what I have lived and learned. I am praying this impartation of present truths will help to prepare you for the Lord. To be prepared for the Lord, you must follow the example of Jesus. He was led by the Spirit into the wilderness to go through the process. When you become prepared for the Master and not for man, the Lord whom you seek will suddenly come to His temple. You are the temple of the Lord. When the Lord prepares you, He prepares you for Himself. He is seeking and searching for those who are seeking for Him. It is written in Malachi 3:1: "*Behold, I will send my messenger and he shall prepare the way before me: and the Lord, whom ye seek, shall suddenly come to his temple, even the messenger of the covenant, whom ye delight in: behold, he shall come, saith the LORD of hosts."*

You are now and you are becoming a people prepared for the Lord. Through every test and trial, you are being made ready for the Lord. The journey has just begun. You are moving in the right direction, the direction of the Word of God renewing your mind.

FOUNDATION OF GOD STANDETH SURE

"Nevertheless the foundation of God standeth sure, having this seal, The Lord knoweth them that are his. And, Let everyone that nameth the name of Christ depart from iniquity." (II Timothy 2:19)

The Lord knows you are His. You must never forget whose you are and who God has called you to be. Don't allow yourself to become frustrated with yourself when you make a mistake; continue on with God. Ministers and saints of God, God knew you before you were born. You are God's building and you have been built upon its foundation. His foundation standeth sure.

The Apostle Paul writes these words in I Corinthians 3:11 and Ephesians 2:20...
"For other foundation can no man lay than that is laid, which is Jesus Christ." (I Corinthians 3:11)

"And are built upon the foundation of the apostles and prophets, Jesus Christ himself being the chief corner stone;" (Ephesians 2:20)

These great men and women of God taught me what their spiritual leaders had taught them. God would allow Bishop Charles Johnson to preach revelatory truths that stirred up a hunger and thirst for more of Christ. As long as he was evangelizing throughout the United States and abroad, that fire kept burning.

When the fall season came, the tent would be taken down again until spring. Bishop saw the people as sheep without a shepherd. When he began pastoring, one day he told me, "Sister Batts, you can never build or establish a church evangelizing." I did not understand fully what he was trying to tell me until years later when he appointed me pastor of his church. There was no voting in or voting out. The bishop had spoken and I was taught that you obey those who had the rule over you for they watch out for your soul. For seven years, I drove what seemed to be hundreds of miles, when it was actually less than fifty miles each way. My husband was active duty military at the time. We had five children whose ages ranged from five through that left me to care for the children and the newly appointed church. The church was located in Southern Pines, NC with a Caucasian bishop until the church was placed in my care. This was in 1984 and in the south. It did not take but a few Sundays of me showing up to preach to cause a once full church to become three- fourths empty.

You may be wondering about my prior pastoral training. I taught a youth, teen and adult Bible study. I ministered in the military gospel service one Sunday morning when the Chaplain was absent. I also ministered for Women Aglow and other services.

Needless to say, my evangelizing did not equip me to pastor a church. (Now that I look back over those seven years, I ask God to forgive me and I ask the few faithful people who remained to forgive me and may God richly bless you.) Each Sunday morning before I preached I gave this announcement, "Your dad is gone I am only babysitting and he will return soon." The young man who is now serving as pastor and bishop is superseding what I could never do.

How I wish I had been told this truth: You may be assigned by man, but you must only look at it as an assignment and not a divine appointment from the Lord. Appointments change, but your divine assignment from the Lord must be fulfilled. You are able to fulfill every divine appointment from the Lord by the grace of God. Grace in ministry is God's enabling power. God will anoint those He has appointed into a position in church. There are no big callings or small callings. Those who have been called by God are fulfilling His divine purpose and God's plan for their lives.

I
ALL FILLED WITH THE HOLY SPIRIT

Acts 2: 1-3
"And when the day of Pentecost was fully come, they were all with one accord in one place. And suddenly there came a sound from heaven as of a rushing mighty wind, and it filled all the house where they were sitting. And there appeared unto them cloven tongues like as of fire, and it sat upon each of them."

Ministers of God and the body of Christ, the first thing that should take place before you enter into ministry is to become a leader in the Word and the work of God. You must be filled with the Holy Ghost. When you are filled with the Holy Ghost you receive power to speak the language of the kingdom. Not only do you talk the language of the kingdom, but you have power to walk the kingdom walk. You will walk as Jesus walked.

We are living in the last days. In the midst of all the tribulation, distress, sickness, heartbreak and sorrow in the world, God is pouring out His Spirit upon all flesh. Those who are in the flesh must repent and receive Jesus as Lord and Savior of their lives. God is not going to remove His hand from you for He loves you and His desire is to bring you into the kingdom.

The outpouring of Holy Spirit is another

demonstration of God's great love for the world. Before the outpouring of the Holy Ghost, God sent His only begotten Son, Jesus, into the world and He died on the cross as payment for the sins of the world. What great love! According to John 3:16-17, we read…

"For God so loved the world that he gave his only begotten Son, that whosoever believeth in him should not perish, but have everlasting life. For God sent not his Son into the world to condemn the world; but that the world through him might be saved."

After Jesus died on the cross and was buried, He rose from the grave and went back to heaven. God's love for the world did not stop there. God was going to continue to demonstrate His love for the human race until Jesus returns on a cloud to catch all of those who received Jesus as Savior and Lord of their lives. Everyone who rejected the Spirit of God when He poured out His Spirit upon all flesh will not be saved. It is God's perfect will that all men be saved. Ministers… you must keep this gospel truth before you continuously. This message is the power of God unto salvation.

I read the gospel of Jesus Christ, but it was not bound about my neck. My mind never became renewed to the fact that every time I preached or taught, every message should conclude with the gospel of Jesus Christ. His gospel gives all men the opportunity to receive Him as Lord and Savior of their life. There is an infilling of the Holy Ghost, but there is also a great outpouring in the last days. How do we know there is an outpouring of the Holy Ghost upon all flesh? God said we should believe it and that settles it.

As God pours out His Spirit upon all flesh, those who are walking in the flesh must believe and receive the outpouring of the Spirit of God. When you reject the Spirit of God, the flesh will continue to control you and manifest its works. In Galatians 5:19-21, the works of the flesh are revealed.

The works of the flesh will hinder the presence and power of God. The whole creation is groaning for a manifestation of the sons of God and the sons of God will carry the presence of God into the people of God. The works of the flesh must be crucified. The Apostle Paul revealed the works of the flesh in Galatians 5:19-21 which read:

"Now the works of the flesh are manifest, which are these; Adultery, fornication, uncleanness, lasciviousness, idolatry, witchcraft, hatred, variance, emulations, wrath, strife, seditions, heresies, envyings, murders, drunkenness, revellings, and such like: of the which I tell you before, as I have also told you in time past, that they which do such things shall not inherit the kingdom of God."

As you are taught the Word of God and you make a choice to obey God's Word, you will begin to produce the fruit of the Spirit in your life. Paul continues on to reveal the fruit of the Spirit. It is God's perfect will for every Holy Spirit-filled Christian to produce the Fruit of the Spirit. The Apostle Paul wrote in Galatians 5:22-23:

"But the fruit of the Spirit is love, joy, peace, longsuffering, gentleness, goodness, faith, meekness, temperance: against such there is no law."

Ministers of God, God has raised you up for such a time as this. As you willingly submit to the will and the Word of God, God will make you and will prepare you for the Lord. After you have been made and then prepared for the Lord, you will be able to be the Lord's minister for His people.

There will be many coming into God's house from the world of darkness, tribulation, pain, suffering and every sin you can find in Webster's Dictionary; will you be ready for them? They will not look or act like sinners of yesterday; these are sinners of today. The sinners of today have knowledge but not know-how.

They have been almost everywhere and have done almost everything at a young age. They are seeking for a demonstration and a manifestation of the power and presence of God. I believe that is one of the reasons we are seeing God to pour out of His Spirit upon all flesh and fleshly men and women are gathering into the house of God like we have never seen before. They are not seeking for entertainers because they have been there, done that and they are void and empty. They are searching for a quickening. They have experienced the high of drugs, alcohol and sex; but that void, empty place was not filled. My question to you ministers is, "Are you ready?" Ready or not, the world is coming into the church.

Will the church remain on the Rock or will it slowly sink into the sand? Jesus knew this day was coming, so Jesus warned us ahead of time when He said, *"…upon this rock I will build my church; and the gates of hell shall not prevail against it."* (Matthew 16:18)

Ministers of God, if you are made ready and prepared for the Lord you will be able to minister by the power and presence of the Holy Ghost, preparing the way for the Lord. When there is a visitation of the Lord in your midst, the Word of God will become Spirit and life. When I speak of God's Word becoming Spirit and life, the breath of God breathed upon God's Word and there will be a revelation of God's Word you have never seen before.

In John 6:63, we read:
"It is the spirit that quickeneth; the flesh profiteth nothing: the words that I speak unto you, they are spirit, and they are life."

Only by the Spirit of God will you be able to receive a revelation of the Word of God and be able to see things you have never seen before. When there is a revelation of the Word of God; Spirit is ministering to Spirit.

II
BELIEVE GOD IS WITH YOU

Believe God is with you and He will lead and guide
you into all truths. You must know the truth of God's
voice by His word. God's word confirms His voice.
In John 16:13, we read:

*"Howbeit when he, the Spirit of truth, is come, he will
guide you into all truth: for he shall not speak of himself;
but whatsoever he shall hear, that shall he speak: and he
will shew you things to come."*

When He, the Spirit of truth is come, you will not
need to ask anyone if He has come. He always leaves a
manifestation of His presence. I did not know when
He visited our land we could prepare ourselves for a
harvest. God visited the land of Bethlehem. We read
of God's divine visitation and their return after they
heard God had visited their land. You do not want to
be where God used to be. When God visits your land,
by His presence and His power you are to prepare
yourself and get ready for a new location in the Spirit.
In Ruth 1:6 &19 we read:

*"Then she arose with her daughters in law that she might
return from the country of Moab: for she had heard in
the country of Moab how that the LORD had visited his
people in giving them bread."*

19 "So they two went until they came to Bethlehem. And it came to pass, when they were come to Bethlehem, that all the city was moved about them, and they said, Is this Naomi?"

III
COMPARING THEMSELVES AMONG THEMSELVES ARE NOT WISE

Never press yourself beyond your measure. When you feel you have pressed yourself beyond your measure you must first of all seek God, wait on His voice and do not try to force those who are too weary for the battle to join in the fight with you. They are too faint to fight. No one told me you could be a Spirit-filled Christian, leader, or minister and become too faint to fight. You can be anointed and appointed and still become too faint to fight. David and his men had pressed themselves beyond their measure in I Samuel chapters 21- 25. David first sought God to find out what he should do after his wife and the wives of his men and their families had been kidnapped. God spoke to him and gave David instructions of what to do in the midst of battle. In 1 Samuel 30:8-10 & 19 we read:

"And David inquired at the LORD, saying, Shall I pursue after this troop? Shall I overtake them? And he answered him...Pursue: for thou shalt surely overtake them, and without fail recover all. So David went, he and the six hundred men that were with him, and came to the brook Besor, where those that were left behind stayed. But David pursued, he and four hundred men: for two hundred abode behind, which were so faint that they could not go over the brook Besor.

19 "And there was nothing lacking to them, neither small nor great, neither sons nor daughters, neither spoil, nor any thing that they had taken to them: David recovered all."

Paul talks about being pressed beyond measure in II Corinthians 1:8-14, which reads:
"For we would not, brethren, have you ignorant of our trouble which came to us in Asia, that we were pressed out of measure, above strength, insomuch that we despaired even of life: But we had the sentence of death in ourselves, that we should not trust in ourselves, but in God which raiseth the dead: Who delivered us from so great a death, and doth deliver: in whom we trust that he will yet deliver us; Ye also helping together by prayer for us, that for the gift bestowed upon us by the means of many persons thanks may be given by many on our behalf. For our rejoicing is this, the testimony of our conscience, that in simplicity and godly sincerity, not with fleshly wisdom, but by the grace of God, we have had our conversation in the world, and more abundantly to you-ward. For we write none other things unto you, than what ye read or acknowledge; and I trust ye shall acknowledge even to the end; As also ye have acknowledged us in part, that we are your rejoicing, even as ye also are ours in the day of the Lord Jesus."

Ministers of God, you cannot be everything to everyone. You must make your calling and election sure. If you do these things you will never fall or be unfruitful in the work and the Word of God. I was not taught this much needed principle by my mentors. It took me many years to learn all that I did that was not of faith was sin. The word "sin" means "I was missing the mark God had set for me.

IV
ABRAHAM BELIEVED GOD

All that is not of faith is sin. The Apostle Paul wrote
in Romans 14:23, "*And he that doubteth is damned if
he eat, because he eateth not of faith: for whatsoever is
not of faith is sin.*"

There are so many in the body of Christ who try to
walk and live by another man's word instead of
waiting to hear the voice of God in His Word. It is
written in Hebrews 3:7-8, which read:

"*Wherefore (as the Holy Ghost saith), today if ye will
hear his voice, harden not your hearts, as in the
provocation, in the day of temptation in the wilderness.*"

A hardened heart is a heart that has not grown in the
Word of God and will limit the power of God to
produce the promise. Your faith cannot and will not
increase if The Word of God does not become hidden
in your heart. If the Word of God is hidden in your
heart, you will not sin against God.

This is a simple message but one of the most
powerful messages that will help you to overcome
every test and trial. Abraham just made his mind up
to believe God. He may have begun with little faith,
but when he arrived at his destination his faith had
increased until he believed if he offered up his son,

God would raise him up again.

Many times we seek after the faith of someone else and overlook the measure God has given to us. If you move by fear instead of faith, you will open the door to doubt and fear. It is up to you to activate your faith by using the measure God has given you I am sorry to say, no one told me God had given me the measure of faith needed for where I was in ministry at that given time. I kept seeking for more of faith when I really did not know what I was in need of. As I moved from glory to glory, from test to test, and from trial to trial, God prepared me as I read His Word I was able to get through every test and trial by faith.

Faith comes, but many times you don't see faith coming until the test or trial is over. In Philippians 4:19 we read:

"But my God shall supply all your needs according to his riches in glory by Christ Jesus."

As Abraham believed, so you must also believe.

V
IF YOU DO NOT GO WITH ME

During my early years of ministry, I must be honest with you. I sought for the approval of man instead of depending on the presence of God. After we have submitted ourselves to those who have the rule over us and have taught us the Word of God, we must not go until we know that God will be with us. The teachings of the men and women of God that he has placed over us is needed for our growth and development. We must know for ourselves that God is with us. We must know that the presence of God is resting upon us. We must come to that place in God that it does not matter what happens in our life; we must know that we are in the perfect will of God and that He is with us. I was thrust into an area of ministry that I knew I was not ready for. I made so many foolish mistakes. The Lord did not allow me to be destroyed, nor did he allow those whom I ministered to be destroyed. My advice to every minister who God has called into ministry is this:1)Submit to your pastors; 2) Allow them to instruct you into the ways of righteousness; 3) Study to show yourselves approved unto God; 4) Be ready to humble yourself and be obedient to those who have the rule over you. If you are not led by the Spirit of God and you do not feel you are ready to be released into the ministry, share your feelings with your pastor. God will move upon your pastor to know

God's timing. While you are waiting on the timing of God, apply 2 Timothy 2:15 to your life which reads: *"Study to shew thyself approved unto God, a workman that needeth not to be ashamed, rightly dividing the word of truth."* God will not be with you unless you are in His timing. Your pastor might see you as being grown in the ministry. He has taken note that you have grown in your knowledge of God and your obedience to him or her; but being grown does not mean you are mature. Maturity comes when the Master has approved you, and the Master will go with you. Moses told God, "If you do not go with me, then let us stay here." In Exodus 33:12-15, we read: *"And Moses said unto the LORD… See, thou sayest unto me, Bring up this people: and thou hast not let me know whom thou wilt send with me. Yet thou hast said, I know thee by name, and thou hast also found grace in my sight. Now therefore, I pray thee, if I have found grace in thy sight, shew me now thy way, that I may know thee, that I may find grace in thy sight: and consider that this nation is thy people. And he said, My presence shall go with thee, and I will give thee rest. And he said unto him, If thy presence go not with me, carry us not up hence."*

Ministers of God who serve in the five-fold ministry – and also all areas of ministry – you must know the voice of God. You must also know when God's presence is with you. Many who have been called into ministry are not familiar with God's presence. If you are not sure about the presence of God, you will need to get my books entitled, The Prayer of Faith and God's Presence, and God's Peace and God's Power.

VI
THERE IS A PROCESS BEFORE GOD WILL GIVE YOU POWER

How I wish my mentors had taught me that there was a process before God would bring me into a place of power! In the midst of your process, there will be pain, but God will hear your cry and give you power to endure and prevail. Don't be afraid to groan! Groaning is not a sign of weakness but a sign of pain. You cannot rush the process. God is not like humanity. He is divinity and He is touched by the feelings of our infirmities.

In Genesis 28:20-21, we read:
"And Jacob vowed a vow, saying, If God will be with me, and will keep me in this way that I go, and will give me bread to eat, and raiment   to   put   on, So that I come again to my father's house in peace; then shall the LORD be my God…"

The Lord will show you He is your God. Ministry is all about God showing you He is your God so that you can take the journey He is sending you on.

Read the following Scriptures… Genesis 29:1
"Then Jacob went on his journey, and came into the land of the people of the east."

Exodus 2:23-25
"And it came to pass in process of time that the king of Egypt died: and the children of Israel sighed by reason of the bondage, and they cried, and their cry came up unto God by reason of the bondage. And God heard their groaning, and God remembered his covenant with Abraham, with Isaac, and with Jacob. And God looked upon the children of Israel, and God had respect unto them."

Genesis 29:1
"Then Jacob went on his journey, and came into the land of the people of the east."

Exodus 2:23-25
"And it came to pass in process of time that the king of Egypt died: and the children of Israel sighed by reason of the bondage, and they cried, and their cry came up unto God by reason of the bondage. And God heard their groaning, and God remembered his covenant with Abraham, with Isaac, and with Jacob. And God looked upon the children of Israel, and God had respect unto them."

Hebrews 4:15
"For we have not an high priest which cannot be touched with the feeling of our infirmities; but was in all points tempted like as we are, yet without sin."

After the process of time God brought Jacob into a place of power with man and with God. In Genesis 32:24-32, we read:

"And Jacob was left alone; and there wrestled a man with him until the breaking of the day. And when he saw that he prevailed not against him, he touched the hollow of his thigh; and the hollow of Jacob's thigh was out of joint, as he wrestled with him. And he said, Let me go, for the day breaketh. And he said, 'I will not let thee go, except thou bless me' And he said unto him, 'What is thy name?' And he said, Jacob. And he said, 'Thy name shall be called no more Jacob, but Israel: for as a prince hast thou power with God and with men, and hast prevailed.' And Jacob asked him, and said, Tell me, I pray thee, thy name. And he said, 'Wherefore is it that thou dost ask after my name?' And he blessed him there. And Jacob called the name of the place Peniel: for I have seen God face to face, and my life is preserved. And as he passed over Penuel the sun rose upon him, and he halted upon his thigh. Therefore the children of Israel eat not of the sinew which shrank, which is upon the hollow of the thigh, unto this day: because he touched the hollow of Jacob's thigh in the sinew that shrank."

Joseph went through the process. He did not know he was going through a process and that it was the leading of the Lord. The feeding of the Lord comes first. You must learn to feed upon the Lord by your eating His Word before you step into the leading of the Lord.

Take time to read of young Joseph's translation from glory to glory in Genesis 37:5-11, which reads:

"And Joseph dreamed a dream, and he told it his brethren: and they hated him yet the more. And he said unto them, Hear, I pray you, this dream which I have dreamed: For, behold, we were binding sheaves in the field, and, lo, my sheaf arose, and also stood upright; and, behold, your sheaves stood round about, and made obeisance to my sheaf. And his brethren said to him, shalt thou indeed reign over us? Or shalt thou indeed have dominion over us? And they hated him yet the more for his dreams and for his words. And he dreamed yet another dream and told it his brethren and said… Behold, I have dreamed a dream more; and behold, the sun and the moon and the eleven stars made obeisance to me. And he told it to his father and to his brethren: and his father rebuked him, and said unto him, what is this dream that thou hast dreamed? Shall I and thy mother and thy brethren indeed come to bow down ourselves to thee to the earth? And his brethren envied him; but his father observed the saying."

Joseph went from the pit, to the prison and the final glory was the manifestation of the dream. There is always a story of suffering and perseverance before the glory of the dream is manifested.

VII
SEPARATION BEFORE A MANIFESTATION

No one told me when I began my walk with the Lord and when I was called into the ministry, that there is always a separation before there is a manifestation of the glory of the Lord. Jesus was separated in the wilderness and went through a season of testing before He entered the temple. It is written in Luke 4:1-13, which reads:

"And Jesus being full of the Holy Ghost returned from Jordan, and was led by the Spirit into the wilderness; 2 Being forty days tempted of the devil. And in those days he did eat nothing: and when they were ended, he afterward hungered. 3 And the devil said unto him, If thou be the Son of God, command this stone that it be made bread. 4 And Jesus answered him, saying, It is written, That man shall not live by bread alone, but by every word of God. 5 And the devil, taking him up into an high mountain, shewed unto him all the kingdoms of the world in a moment of time. 6 And the devil said unto him, All this power will I give thee, and the glory of them: for that is delivered unto me; and to whomsoever I will I give it. 7 If thou therefore wilt worship me, all shall be thine. 8 And Jesus answered and said unto him, Get thee behind me, Satan: for it is written, Thou shalt worship the Lord thy God, and him only shalt thou serve. 9 And he brought him to Jerusalem, and set him on a pinnacle of the temple, and said unto him, If thou be the Son of God, cast thyself down from hence: 10 For it is written, He shall give his angels charge over thee, to keep thee: 11 And in their hands they shall bear thee up, lest at any time thou dash thy

foot against a stone 12 And Jesus answering said unto him, It is said, Thou shalt not tempt the Lord thy God. 13 And when the devil had ended all the temptation, he departed from him for a season."

After Jesus' season of being tempted in the wilderness, He was ready for ministry in the Synagogue. Jesus, the Son of God had to go through His season of testing. We must also follow the example of Jesus, the Son of God. In Luke 4:14-19, we read:

"And Jesus returned in the power of the Spirit into Galilee: and there went out a fame of him through all the region round about. 15 And he taught in their synagogues, being glorified of all. 16 And he came to Nazareth, where he had been brought up: and, as his custom was, he went into the synagogue on the Sabbath day, and stood up for to read. 17 And there was delivered unto him the book of the prophet Esaias. And when he had opened the book, he found the place where it was written, 18 The Spirit of the Lord is upon me, because he hath anointed me to preach the gospel to the poor; he hath sent me to heal the brokenhearted, to preach deliverance to the captives, and recovering of sight to the blind, to set at liberty them that are bruised, 19 To preach the acceptable year of the Lord."

This is the acceptable year of the Lord. Up until now, the kingdom of heaven suffered violence and the violent took it by force. Through the power of Holy Spirit, we will decree this is the acceptable year of our Lord

VIII
SEARCH THE SCRIPTURES

"Search the scriptures; for in them ye think ye have eternal life: and they are they which testify of me." (John 5:39)

The late Overseer, Pastor Seles Smith, spoke into my life over and over again until the Lord raptured her. She said, "You have always sought every answer to all questions in God's Word. That is why I have continued to bring you questions for which I am unable to find the answers. For over thirty years you have searched God's Word for answers. Never stop doing that!"

My mentors thought I knew this truth because God was using me to preach and teach His word. Due to my fear of God and my respect for Him, I never wanted to step into a gray area so I considered myself as ignorant to every question anyone would ask me. It did not matter if it was a question pertaining to the Word of God or the affairs of someone's daily life; I considered myself ignorant to all matters. Due to my ignorance, over these thirty years that I pastured and ministered, I still consider myself as not knowing everything that I should know. I am still a fool for Christ's sake. My dependency is upon Jesus, through the power of Holy Spirit and the Word of God. Thank you, Overseer Seles Smith, who was only Sister

Seles Smith when she spoke into my life. My words to every born-again son of God are: "The opinion of man will change from season to season, but the mind and word of the Master will never change. He is the living Word of God."

Meditate on the following Scriptures... John 1:1-2

"In the beginning was the Word, and the Word was with God, and the Word was God. 2 The same was in the beginning with God."

Hebrews 13:8
"Jesus Christ the same yesterday, and today, and forever."

Revelation 1:1-2
"The Revelation of Jesus Christ, which God gave unto him, to shew unto his servants things which must shortly come to pass; and he sent and signified it by his angel unto his servant John: 2 Who bare record of the word of God, and of the testimony of Jesus Christ, and of all things that he saw."

IX
GRACE ACCORDING TO THE MEASURE OF THE GIFT

How I wish I had known that there were at least thirty- two gifts in the body of Christ; congregational & governmental. There are at least twenty-seven that are congregational and five that are governmental.

When I began my walk with the Lord and disciplined myself to study His Word, I learned over the years that every member in the body of Christ was given a gift. During the early years of my ministry, we were taught that if you were called by God into the ministry, you were an apostle, prophet, evangelist, pastor or teacher. Outside of these ministries you were a member in the congregation. In John 5:39, we read:
"Search the scriptures; for in them ye think ye have eternal life: and they are they which testify of me."

After searching the scriptures and studying scripture based materials of other men and women of God, I became enlightened to the fact that there were other gifts Christ Jesus had given to the body of Christ. I began a leadership and minister's class on Wednesday from 10:30 a.m. to 12:30 p.m. teaching the body of Christ about the gifts that had been given to the body of Christ. Not only have these gifts been given to the church – which is His body – but God's enabling grace helps us operate in these gifts. In Romans 12:3-8 and Ephesians 4:7, we read:

"For I say, through the grace given unto me, to every man that is among you, not to think of himself more highly than he ought to think; but to think soberly, according as God hath dealt to every man the measure of faith. 4 For as we have many members in one body, and all members have not the same office: 5 So we, being many, are one body in Christ, and every one members one of another. 6 Having then gifts differing according to the grace that is given to us, whether prophecy, let us prophesy according to the proportion of faith; 7 Or ministry, let us wait on our ministering: or he that teacheth, on teaching; 8 Or he that exhorteth, on exhortation: he that giveth, let him do it with simplicity; he that ruleth, with diligence; he that sheweth mercy, with cheerfulness."

"But unto every one of us is given grace according to the measure of the gift of Christ." (Ephesians 4:7)

If you desire an independent study on the gifts of the Spirit, you will need to read the book God directed me to write a few years ago entitled, God's Leaders, God's Ministers, and God's Way. There is a year of CDs taught on that subject from my Wednesday class. I know they will bless your life as they have blessed mine, as I delivered these truths to the body of Christ.

X
HE IS THE HEAD OF THE BODY

My mentors taught me about Jesus, and I thank God for allowing them to bring me into a closer walk with God. I knew then and I know now, that I must not destroy the foundation of Jesus and the apostles' doctrine they put into my life. I also know that I must continue to build upon that foundation.

I was almost drawn into dead works. Dead works are the works that set up religion and denominational walls. How I wish they had taught me that we are all members of His body and He is the head of the church. In Colossians 1:17-20 and Ephesians 5:23, we read:

"And he is before all things, and by him all things consist. 18 And he is the head of the body, the church: who is the beginning, the firstborn from the dead; that in all things he might have the preeminence. 19 For it pleased the Father that in him should all fullness dwell; 20 And, having made peace through the blood of his cross, by him to reconcile all things unto himself; by him, I say, whether they be things in earth, or things in heaven."

"For the husband is the head of the wife, even as Christ is the head of the church: and he is the Savior of the body." (Ephesians 5:23)

The revelation is that Christ is the head of the church. The Head is seated on the right hand of God. The right hand speaks of all power and authority. In Acts 2:30-34 and Hebrews 1:13, we read:

"Therefore being a prophet, and knowing that God had sworn with an oath to him, that of the fruit of his loins, according to the flesh, he would raise up Christ to sit on his throne; 31 He seeing this before spake of the resurrection of Christ, that his soul was not left in hell, neither his flesh did see corruption. 32 This Jesus hath God raised up, whereof we all are witnesses.
33 Therefore being by the right hand of God exalted, and having received of the Father the promise of the Holy Ghost, he hath shed forth this, which ye now see and hear. 34 For David is not ascended into the heavens: but he saith himself, The LORD said unto my Lord, Sit thou on my right hand..."

"But to which of the angels said he at any time, sit on my right hand, until I make thine enemies thy footstool?" (Hebrews 1:13)

Body of Christ, the church is in the earth. Our divine assignment from God is to make our calling and election sure by knowing our gift and calling. Peter wrote in 2 Peter 1:10, *"Wherefore the rather, brethren, give diligence to make your calling and election sure: for if ye do these thing, ye shall never fall..."*

I know many biblical scholars use this scripture when referring to the natural Israel. God spoke in my heart one day as I was reading this scripture and said, "Dorothy, this scripture is also for my church, the body of Christ. Many are becoming weary in their waiting, because they do not know where they fit in the body of Christ. Tell My people, I placed a gift and calling within them before the foundation of the world. I placed ministers, pastors, and teachers in their lives to perfect and mature them for the work of the ministry. Tell My children not to become pressed beyond their measure. They will know when they are within their measure. Then they have my peace to move forward in their gift and to do the work of the ministry. If there is no peace, stand still until you see the salvation of the Lord."

Jesus said in John 14:27, "*Peace I leave with you, my peace I give unto you: not as the world giveth, give unto you. Let not your heart be troubled, neither let it be afraid.*"

The Apostle Paul wrote in I Corinthians 12:27- 28 these words:

"*Now ye are the body of Christ, and members in particular. 28 And God hath set some in the church, first apostles, secondarily prophets, thirdly teachers, after that miracles, then gifts of healings, helps, governments, diversities of tongues.*"

XI
BE ESTABLISHED IN THE PRESENT TRUTH

I was not taught by my 0mentors and leaders that immaturity was the major cause of leaders and ministers falling into the pitfalls of the devil. I was taught the Holy Ghost is a keeper.

If you have the Holy Ghost you do not need anything else; that is present and future truth. But we must begin our walk and talk with God in present truth. In 2 Peter 1:12, we read: "*Wherefore I will not be negligent to put you always in remembrance of these things, though ye know them, and be established in the present truth.*"

I was not taught that there is a road every born-again Christian must travel down to enter that place of future truth. Until each of us comes to the place in our lives that we have grown to the measure and power of future truth, we must learn to receive, believe, and hold fast to the Word of God so that we can grow. In 1 Peter 1:1-3, we read:

"*Peter, an apostle of Jesus Christ, to the strangers scattered throughout Pontus, Galatia, Cappadocia, Asia, and Bithynia, 2 Elect according to the foreknowledge of God the Father, through sanctification of the Spirit, unto obedience and sprinkling of the blood of Jesus Christ:*

39

Grace unto you, and peace, be multiplied. 3 Blessed be the God and Father of our Lord Jesus Christ, which according to his abundant mercy hath begotten us again unto a lively hope by the resurrection of Jesus Christ from the dead."

When you have gone through the process of growth and you have come to the fullness of the measure of the stature of Christ, then you are ready to be placed in a position of leadership and ministry. "For the perfecting (maturing, furnishing with the Word of God, thoroughly completing and equipping before one is positioned in leadership and ministry) of the saints for the work of the ministry and edifying." The Greek translation of this word will enable you to better understand your mission from the Master.

Edifying – (Greek "oikodomeo") to construct, to confirm; also means a confirmation; preparing a place for the dwelling of its occupancy.

We are a people being prepared for the Lord. The Lord whom ye seek shall suddenly come to His temple; but the temple must be prepared for Him. My mentors did not teach these truths to me. They taught me the things they had learned from their teachers about the body of Christ.

The message of leadership and ministry written in Ephesians 4:12-16 prepared the saints for the work of the ministry. This is good to be prepared for the work of the ministry. While you are being prepared for the work of the ministry, you must also prepare yourself for the Lord. Paul writes in Ephesians 4:12-16 these words:

"For the perfecting of the saints, for the work of the ministry, for the edifying of the body of Christ: 13 Till we all come in the unity of the faith, and of the knowledge of the Son of God, unto a perfect man, unto the measure of the stature of the fullness of Christ: 14 That we henceforth be no more children, tossed to and fro, and carried about with every wind of doctrine, by the sleight of men, and cunning craftiness, whereby they lie in wait to deceive; 15 But speaking the truth in love, may grow up into him in all things, which is the head, even Christ: 16 From whom the whole body fitly joined together and compacted by that which every joint supplieth, according to the effectual working in the measure of every part, maketh increase of the body unto the edifying of itself in love."

We have spent years preparing the body of Christ for the ministry instead of preparing the body for the Master. When I speak of preparing them for the ministry, I know from experience. I have set my ministry staff in place to minister the Word of God. That is good and it must be done. But we, as pastors, teachers, apostles, prophets and evangelists, should place more emphasis on preparing them for the Lord instead of making sure they are prepared for the ministry. It should be the Master before the ministry. If you have been prepared for the Master, you will not have any problems doing the work of the ministry.

XII

PARTAKERS OF THE DIVINE NATURE

How I wish my mentors had told me that it is God's perfect will that I become a partaker of His divine nature.

To govern is to bring everything that is out of order back into the order of God. The only way you are going to have that power and authority is to learn the things your teachers and mentors did not know when they began to walk with God. Isaiah 1:19 reads:

"If ye be willing and obedient, ye shall eat the good of the land..."

This scripture and all scriptures are true to fact. The Word of God will stand forever. My prayer for every born-again Christian – and all those who have been called into leadership and ministry – is that they will be able to take truths and begin applying them to their life. Believing God, through the Holy Ghost, will develop His divine nature in you so that you will be able to recognize Satan's pitfalls.

As each believer becomes knowledgeable of the pitfalls of Satan, they will not become ensnared with his deceptive tactics. It is God's perfect will that you never fall. Peter writes of the attributes that produce a life that has been rooted and grounded in the Word of God from the first day you gave your life to Christ. In 2 Peter 1:3- 11, we read:

"According as his divine power hath given unto us all things that pertain unto life and godliness, through the knowledge of him that hath called us to glory and virtue: 4 Whereby are given unto us exceeding great and precious promises: that by these ye might be partakers of the divine nature, having escaped the corruption that is in the world through lust. 5 And beside this, giving all diligence, add to your faith virtue; and to virtue knowledge; 6 And to knowledge temperance; and to temperance patience; and to patience godliness; 7 And to godliness brotherly kindness; and to brotherly kindness charity. 8 For if these things be in you, and abound, they make you that ye shall neither be barren nor unfruitful in the knowledge of our Lord Jesus Christ. 9 But he that lacketh these things is blind, and cannot see afar off, and hath forgotten that he was purged from his old sins. 10 Wherefore the rather, brethren, give diligence to make your calling and election sure: for if ye do these things, ye shall never fall: 11 For so an entrance shall be ministered unto you abundantly into the everlasting kingdom of our Lord and Savior Jesus Christ."

When we were redeemed and God sent His Holy Spirit to live in us, we possessed the same Spirit that raised Jesus from the dead. In Romans 8:10-11 and Acts 1:8, we read:

"And if Christ be in you, the body is dead because of sin; but the Spirit is life because of righteousness. 11 But if the Spirit of him that raised up Jesus from the dead dwell in you, he that raised up Christ from the dead shall also quicken your mortal bodies by his Spirit that dwelleth in you."

"But ye shall receive power, after that the Holy Ghost is come upon you: and ye shall be witnesses unto me both in Jerusalem, and in all Judaea, and in Samaria, and unto the uttermost part of the earth." (Acts 1:8)

The indwelling power of Holy Spirit can keep you from falling as you yield yourself to the productiveness of the fruit of righteousness. We have been given all things pertaining to life and godliness.

Begin this very moment becoming a partaker of the divine nature of our Lord and Savior Jesus Christ. If you do, you will not need to wait until you get my age and then look back over the years you spent trying to be like Jesus instead of knowing you are a Son of God. All I needed to do was to take my time growing.

In my younger days it was what you did for God that made you holy. That was taught among the apostles, prophets, evangelists, pastors and teachers. It is not what we do that makes us holy but it is submitting our lives to our Lord and Savior Jesus Christ and allowing Him to lead and guide us into all truths.

Jesus came and brought us into a new and living way. Through the power of Holy Spirit and our knowledge and obedience to the Word of God, we are in a new and living way knowing Christ and growing into the fullness of the measure of Christ. He has brought joy and peace in the Holy Ghost.

Now, I obey Him and do what He says because I love Him. The love for my Lord and Savior is the motivating force. Grace and His blood are active every day of my life.

Have I lived a holy life and never did anything wrong? Yes! I learned from my mistakes and failure but the grace of God and His love for humanity has brought me this far. I know what Jesus meant when He said,

"Yet I will rejoice in the LORD, I will joy in the God of my salvation." (Habakkuk 3:18)

I pray these truths will bless you. I have lived and walked them through my fifty years of being a born-again Christian and my in thirty years of ministry.

XIII
GOD IS NOT ASHAMED TO BE CALLED
THEIR GOD

To summarize everything that I have written, I impart this truth into your life: God began a good work in me and is completing it until the day of the Lord. The same God who began a good work in me is also the same God who began a good work in you.

As for me, I have learned to forget the things that are behind and press towards the mark of the high calling in Christ Jesus. If I miss the mark today, I thank God that I have faith in Him that He will complete the things He has begun in me. Paul wrote in Philippians 3:14, "I press toward the mark for the prize of the high calling of God in Christ Jesus."

God has no respect of persons. He began a good work in you. That work began when He sent Jesus to redeem us from the curse of the Law. What great love He has shown for humanity. Meditate on the following Scriptures:

Romans 2:11
"For there is no respect of persons with God."

Philemon 1:6
"Being confident of this very thing that he which hath

begun a good work in you will perform it until the day of Jesus Christ."

John 3:16-17
"For God so loved the world, that he gave his only begotten Son, that whosoever believeth in him should not perish, but have everlasting life.17 For God sent not his Son into the world to condemn the world; but that the world through him might be saved."

God did not stop there. He did not wait until we were trying to be good enough; but while we were yet sinners, Christ died for us.

Romans 5:8 reads:

"But God commendeth his love toward us, in that, while we were yet sinners, Christ died for us."

Now that you know these things, begin to live a life of victory, peace and power so if you happen to make a mistake today or if the enemy trips you up, do not allow him to bring a spirit of condemnation upon you. You must repent of all known sins. Forsake sin and forget the things that are behind. We read in Lamentations 3:21-26 these words:

"This I recall to my mind, therefore have I hope. 22 It is of the LORD's mercies that we are not consumed, because his compassions fail not. 23 They are new every

morning: great is thy faithfulness. 24The LORD is my portion, saith my soul; therefore will I hope in him. 25 The LORD is good unto them that wait for him, to the soul that seeketh him. 26 It is good that a man should both hope and quietly wait for the salvation of the LORD."

Now that you know these things, believe them and enjoy your life with the Lord. Meditate on these scriptures in Hebrews 10:15-38 which read:

"Whereof the Holy Ghost also is a witness to us: for after that he had said before, 16 This is the covenant that I will make with them after those days, saith the Lord, I will put my laws into their hearts, and in their minds will I write them; 17 And their sins and iniquities will I remember no more. 18 Now where remission of these is, there is no more offering for sin.19 Having therefore, brethren, boldness to enter into the holiest by the blood of Jesus, 20 By a new and living way, which he hath consecrated for us, through the veil, that is to say, his flesh; 21 And having an high priest over the house of God; 22 Let us draw near with a true heart in full assurance of faith, having our hearts sprinkled from an evil conscience, and our bodies washed with pure water. 23 Let us hold fast the profession of our faith without wavering; (for he is faithful that promised;) 24 And let us consider one another to provoke unto love and to good works: 25 Not forsaking the assembling of ourselves together, as the manner of some is; but exhorting one another: and so much the more, as ye see the day

approaching. 26 For if we sin willfully after that we have received the knowledge of the truth, there remaineth no more sacrifice for sins,27 But a certain fearful looking for of judgment and fiery indignation, which shall devour the adversaries. 28 He that despised Moses' law died without mercy under two or three witnesses: 29 Of how much sorer punishment, suppose ye, shall he be thought worthy, who hath trodden underfoot the Son of God, and hath counted the blood of the covenant, wherewith he was sanctified, an unholy thing, and hath done despite unto the Spirit of grace? 30 For we know him that hath said, Vengeance belongeth unto me, I will recompense, saith the Lord. And again, The Lord shall judge his people. 31 It is a fearful thing to fall into the hands of the living God. 32 But call to remembrance the former days, in which, after ye were illuminated, ye endured a great fight of afflictions; 33 Partly, whilst ye were made a gazing stock both by reproaches and afflictions; and partly, whilst ye became companions of them that were so used. 34 For ye had compassion of me in my bonds, and took joyfully the spoiling of your goods, knowing in yourselves that ye have in heaven a better and an enduring substance. 35 Cast not away therefore your confidence, which hath great recompence of reward. 36 For ye have need of patience, that, after ye have done the will of God, ye might receive the promise. 37 For yet a little while, and he that shall come will come, and will not tarry 38 Now the just shall live by faith: but if any man draw back, my soul shall have no pleasure in him."

I did not know during the early years of walking
with God and being in the ministry that you can
have great faith and still not receive the promise. It
was later in life that God revealed this truth to me.
You are never to stop believing God for His promises
to be fulfilled in your life and the lives of your family
and friends. If they are walking upright before God
and they have received Jesus as Lord and Savior of
their lives, they must continue to hold fast to their
confidence in God knowing He will give them great
recompense of reward. Ruth 2:12 reads, *"The LORD
recompense they work, and a full reward be given thee
of the LORD God of Israel, under whose wings thou art
come to trust."*

To the children of God, His mercies and His grace
are new every day. You might have sinned or tripped
up yesterday. When you asked God to forgive you for
your sins, the blood of Jesus washed you clean. Each
day God's mercies are shown upon you and me and
we are justified as we come boldly before the throne
of God.

*"Let us therefore come boldly unto the throne of grace,
that we may obtain mercy, and find grace to help in
time of need." (Hebrews 4:16)*

The word justified means the blood of Jesus has
washed us and made us clean; just as if we had not
sinned. We come into the presence of God when we

pray and we make our request known. That is just what the patriarchs of faith did. Take a few minutes to learn what Holy Spirit revealed about each of the patriarchs in Hebrews 11:3-12 which read:

"Through faith we understand that the worlds were framed by the word of God, so that things which are seen were not made of things which do appear. 4 By faith Abel offered unto God a more excellent sacrifice than Cain, by which he obtained witness that he was righteous, God testifying of his gifts: and by it he being dead yet speaketh. 5 By faith Enoch was translated that he should not see death; and was not found, because God had translated him: for before his translation he had this testimony, that he pleased God. 6 But without faith it is impossible to please him: for he that cometh to God must believe that he is, and that he is a rewarder of them that diligently seek him. 7 By faith Noah, being warned of God of things not seen as yet, moved with fear, prepared an ark to the saving of his house; by the which he condemned the world, and became heir of the righteousness which is by faith. 8 By faith Abraham, when he was called to go out into a place which he should after receive for an inheritance, obeyed; and he went out, not knowing whither he went. 9 By faith he sojourned in the land of promise, as in a strange country, dwelling in tabernacles with Isaac and Jacob, the heirs with him of the same promise: 10 For he looked for a city which hath foundations, whose builder and maker is God. 11 Through faith also Sara herself received strength to conceive seed, and was delivered of a child when she was past age, because she judged him faithful who had promised. 12 Therefore sprang there even of one, and him as good as dead, so many as the stars of the sky in multitude, and as the sand which is by the sea shore innumerable."

In Hebrews 11:13, the Holy Spirit begins to reveal another side of faith. "*These all died in faith, not having received the promises, but having seen them afar off, and were persuaded of them, and embraced them, and confessed that they were strangers and pilgrims on the earth.*"

As I think back over my years of walking with the Lord, I cannot remember anyone teaching me that you can die in faith without receiving the promise. Many tried to explain why a spirit-filled saint who did not reach the age of twenty, died without living out their full life. Their reasoning was that God took them while they were a Christian because He knew that they might not have been able to live a Christian life until Jesus returned. What about a spirit-filled mother, married, with young children and a husband who loved them very much? What about a father who ran back into a burning house to save his children?

Those who are God's children, died in faith. There is still a thief. He goes around as a roaring lion seeking whom he may devour. John 10:10 reads: "*The thief cometh not, but for to steal, and to kill, and to destroy: I am come that they might have life, and that they might have it more abundantly.*"

Due to the fall of Adam, and him giving Satan the dominion he had received from God, the devil goes throughout the world seeking whom he may devour. *"Be sober, be vigilant; because the adversary the devil, as a roaring lion, walketh about, seeking whom he may devour." (I Peter 5:8)*

This is not the end of the story. Jesus comes where the devil has brought death and translated God's children from death, sickness and pain into eternal life. Until He returns and destroys the last enemy, which is death, we must hold fast to the confession of our faith until the end, for God is a faithful God. Meditate on the following Scriptures which read:

I Corinthians 15:26
"The last enemy that shall be destroyed is death."

Hebrews 10:23
"Let us hold fast the profession of our faith without wavering; (for he is faithful that promised)."

Deuteronomy 7:9
"Know therefore that the LORD thy God, he is God, which keepeth covenant and mercy with them that love him and keep his commandments to a thousand generations."

Before one of my spiritual sons went on to be with the Lord, he told me, "Mom, it is all about purpose." We are here to fulfill the purpose of God. I have learned over the years, when many children of God go

on to be with the Lord at a young age, they have
fulfilled their purpose. God showed them a city. They
would rather be in the city of God instead of being in
the country of man.

I give this message to you because in my early years of
walking with God and my early years of ministry, I
never knew these things. I encourage you to hold fast
to your profession of faith until the end for God is
faithful. Give yourself time to study the Scriptures.
When you study you are preparing yourself for a
visitation and revelation from the Lord. I know these
truths will bless you and cause your faith to grow
exceedingly. Hold fast to them and never forget God
is with you. When the day comes, He will show you
His city, which the Builder and Maker are. Your
desire will be to leave your country and follow Him to
His city. Even so, come Lord Jesus come.

In Hebrews 11:10, 13-16 we read:
*"For he looked for a city which hath foundations, whose
builder and maker is God."*

"These all died in faith, not having received the
promises, but having seen them afar off, and were
persuaded of them, and embraced them, and
confessed that they were strangers and pilgrims on the
earth. 14 For they that say such things declare plainly
that they seek a country. 15 And truly, if they had
been mindful of that country from whence they came

out, they might have had opportunity to have returned. 16 But now they desire a better country, that is, an heavenly: wherefore God is not ashamed to be called their God: for he hath prepared for them a city."

God has begun a good work in you and His desire is that He can work through you to manifest His power and glory. Through the power of Holy Spirit, you can be an overcomer. It does not matter if you are in a valley of heartaches and pain. You must walk with God through the valley until you reach the mountain. Through your valley journey, God will cause people you once walked with to take a detour. There isn't anything wrong with you. It's just that everyone who began with you does not have the same desire to make the sacrifice to serve the Savior. It is a journey and it is a road of suffering. But it is also a journey of faith in God, righteousness, joy, peace and power to fulfill the promises of God.

I was not taught that there are seasons for relationships. God will bring people into your life for a season. When the season has ended, you must move forward with God into the next season. If you do not move forward, God will cause you to go through an Abraham and Lot encounter.

It is at the altar of God that seasons and people will change if they are not pillars God has placed in your life. Lot was not one of

Abram's pillars. In Genesis 13:3-11 we read:

"And he went on his journeys from the south even to Bethel, unto the place where his tent had been at the beginning, between Bethel and Hai; 4 Unto the place of the altar, which he had made there at the first: and there Abram called on the name of the LORD. 5 And Lot also, which went with Abram, had flocks, and herds, and tents. 6 And the land was not able to bear them, that they might dwell together: for their substance was great, so that they could not dwell together. 7 And there was a strife between the herdmen of Abram's cattle and the herdmen of Lot's cattle: and the Canaanite and the Perizzite dwelled then in the land. 8 And Abram said unto Lot, Let there be no strife, I pray thee, between me and thee, and between my herdmen and thy herdmen; for we be brethren. 9 Is not the whole land before thee? separate thyself, I pray thee, from me: if thou wilt take the left hand, then I will go to the right; or if thou depart to the right hand, then I will go to the left. 10 And Lot lifted up his eyes, and beheld all the plain of Jordan, that it was well watered everywhere, before the LORD destroyed Sodom and Gomorrah, even as the garden of the LORD, like the land of Egypt, as thou comest unto Zoar. 11 Then Lot chose him all the plain of Jordan; and Lot journeyed east: and they separated themselves the one from the other."

Lot's season was over. Abram did not try to convince Lot to continue to go with him until he arrived at the place God was leading him. There must be a separation before there is a visitation of the Lord. It is at the altar of the Lord, during prayer and sacrifice, that you will receive your visitation.

After the visitation there will be an impartation of faith. Your faith in the promises of God and the power of Holy Spirit will give you the power of God to prevail and continue on your journey.

I was not taught people and ministries are placed in your life for a season. Since I was not taught this truth, I tried to hold on to those who had been a blessing to me by depositing into my life.
It took me years to realize and there wasn't anything wrong with me. They were just sent for a reason and that season had to change. They gave way to pillars that were planted in my life by almighty God.

How I thank God for the pillars He sent into my life at a time when I thought I would crumble under pressure. They united with me. Take note, they did not ask me what denomination I was affiliated with. They knew I was a member of the body of Christ. Again, I would like to say thank you, to all the pillars God placed in my life over the past thirty years of ministry.

I dedicate this book to my children, grandchildren, friends, Outreach for Jesus Church family, and all the apostles, prophets, evangelists, pastors, and teachers. God had a friend, whose name was Abraham. God has blessed me and placed friends in my life.

All of you have been a blessing in my life. You have planted into my life and now I pray that I have written divine truths that will bless you.

"But I have prayed for thee that thy faith fail not: and when thou art converted, strengthen thy brethren." (Luke 22:32)

CHAPTER I - Notes

CHAPTERS II & III - Notes

CHAPTER IV - Notes

CHAPTER V - Notes

CHAPTER VI – Notes

CHAPTER VII - Notes

CHAPTER VIII – Notes

CHAPTER IX - Notes

CHAPTER X & XI – Notes

CHAPTER XII - Notes

CHAPTER XIII – Notes

"That I might know Him and the power of his resurrection, and the fellowship of his sufferings, being made conformable unto his death; if by any means I might attain unto the resurrection of the dead. Not as though I had already attained, either were already perfect: but I follow after, if that I may apprehend that for which also I am apprehended of Christ Jesus."
Philippians 3:10-12

Dr. Dorothy Batts has traveled four times to Africa, traveled to Korea, Germany, Hawaii and throughout the United States of America preaching and teaching the gospel of Jesus Christ. God moved upon her by His Spirit anointing her with prophetic, apostolic anointing her revealing many truths from His Word. The Word of God becomes Spirit and Life.

God has anointed and appointed Pastor Batts to preach the gospel of Jesus Christ to the world and to equip and mature the saints and ministers to do the work of the ministry (Ephesians 4: 1-32).

God has favored Pastor Batts. Her name appears in the Library of Congress for Who's Who among Women in the United States and Who's Who among Women in the World in 2017. She is the first Black woman to be the founder and president of an accredited Bible College in Hope Mills, North

Carolina as well as a Word of God Spirit and Life School of Discipleship, Leadership and Ministry. God is continuing to open doors for her to teach and preach the gospel of Jesus Christ in conferences, conventions revivals, and seminars. She is the writer of many Bible study manuals, prayer books and books containing messages from the Lord. When asked about her favorite scripture, she says she loves the entire Bible, the New Testament is her most desired and she loves the scripture, Philippians 3:10-12.

www.ingramcontent.com/pod-product-compliance
Lightning Source LLC
Chambersburg PA
CBHW060145050426
42448CB00010B/2313